YOUR KNOWLEDGE H

- We will publish your bachelor's and master's thesis, essays and papers

- Your own eBook and book - sold worldwide in all relevant shops

- Earn money with each sale

Upload your text at www.GRIN.com
and publish for free

Bibliographic information published by the German National Library:

The German National Library lists this publication in the National Bibliography; detailed bibliographic data are available on the Internet at http://dnb.dnb.de .

Imprint:

Copyright © 2016 GRIN Verlag, Open Publishing GmbH
Print and binding: Books on Demand GmbH, Norderstedt Germany
ISBN: 9783668574984

This book at GRIN:

http://www.grin.com/en/e-book/380879/intercultural-product-communication-an-assessment-of-consumer-electronic

Patrizio Basso

Intercultural Product Communication. An Assessment of Consumer Electronic Products in India and China

GRIN Publishing

GRIN - Your knowledge has value

Since its foundation in 1998, GRIN has specialized in publishing academic texts by students, college teachers and other academics as e-book and printed book. The website www.grin.com is an ideal platform for presenting term papers, final papers, scientific essays, dissertations and specialist books.

Visit us on the internet:

http://www.grin.com/

http://www.facebook.com/grincom

http://www.twitter.com/grin_com

Index of Contents

List of Abbreviations

CPU	Central Processing Unit
PC	Personal Computer
IT	Information Technology
USP	Unique Selling Proposition
R&D	Research & Development
KPI	Key Performance Indicator
PS4	PlayStation4®
ICT	Information and communication technology
CEO	Chief executive officer
4K	Video format resolution with 4,000 horizontal Pixels
DVD	Digital versatile Disc
MP4	MPEG-4
CD	Compact disc
PDI	Power Distance Index
UAI	Uncertainty Avoidance Index
US	United States (of America)
MS-DOS	Microsoft Disk Operating System
BASIC	Beginners All-Purpose Symbolic Instruction Code
IBM	International Business Machines
IPO	Initial Public Offering
PDA	Personal Digital Assistant
E3	Electronic Entertainment Expo
B2C	Brand to Customer
ROI	Return on Investment

List of Figures

1. Introduction

Once one has been to the USA, Italy, Germany, other foreign countries or even China or India, one travels with subconscious stereotypes and prejudices. In consequence of educational background, advertisement, friends and other influences cultural imaginations originate without doing it willful. Now to fit the real cultural requirements one has to study the culture in detail.

To lead into this topic, this thesis examines the product communication in consideration of different cultural circumstances and the development of cultural adaption.

This first chapter outlines the general problem, which international and global action organizations have by facing foreign cultures. The problems guide inevitable to the relevance for economy and the mentioned organizations. Due to the work with and for human beings, also limitations are topic.

The second chapter is devoted to product communication, as part of the marketing mix and under reflection of the pressure triangle.

Chapter 3 is dedicated to the countries India and China. The focus will be set on their cultures, as well as the specific markets.

The fourth chapter illustrates the intercultural product communication based on the observations of the companies Sony, Microsoft, Samsung and Apple. Their products PS4, Xbox One, Galaxy S6 Edge+ and IPhone 6S Plus, will be referred to each core strategy and the cultural characteristics in China respectively India.

After the summary of the observations, which includes the results, as well as a discussion and economic and corporate recommendations in chapter 5, the sixth and last chapter gives an outlook and the conclusion.

1.1. Problem Discussion

Developing new products means not only having an idea of necessities human beings
have, neither being a creative brain. The products if new or not will be promoted on
every market one wants to be present. Moreover, every market has its idiosyncrasies.
But not the specific industrial sector, but also every nation, every town, every communi-
ty and every human (Schönenstein, 2015).

To maximize the turnover besides revenue, global organizations have to concentrate on
their core strategies and how to implement these strategies by adapting cultural circumstances and characteristics. Nevertheless, every human being has a different cultural
identity and is member of diverse social and cultural groups (Shater, 2012). To give an
example of an average man: a thirty years old man, living in Cologne, has Italian and
German roots, is roman-catholic, likes soccer – playing and watching, watches superhe-
ro movies, hears Hip Hop and Electro, works for a postal service provider, and so on.
The mentioned profile could be divided into at least eleven social and/or cultural groups
– to give an impression.

Now, where in market shall an organization place itself and which social or cultural
group does the organization want to address with their product communication? Moreover, how does the communication fit into their core strategy?

1.2. Practical Relevance

The relevance – especially the practical – is to get knowledge about customer's preferences. Industries and organization does not want to pay useless money for advertise-
ments, posters or spots without targeting their focus groups. Targeting the focus groups
means to segment people into specific groups. Religion, nationality, age, gender and
every other thinkable social group can divide these groups.

Especially for global acting companies these segmenting is important, as they need to
know how the groups response to the promotion and if an adaption of various cultural
specifications is necessary. Not only in one country, but also worldwide. Due to this fact,
it is even more difficult to particularize the focus groups, because they need not be built
similar in several countries.

On top of relevance question is to minimize costs and maximize revenue by communicate the correct product for the exact segmented group at least effort. This point will be picked up in several chapters, but in more detail in chapter 2.2.

1.3.   Limitation of Research

Due to the uniqueness of human beings, their thoughts and preferences, it is impossible to explore each peculiarity, which could be an interesting point while creating, producing or communicating a product. Furthermore, it does not make sense. An organization will not produce a product for only one person. The limitation frame is given by logical conditions – mentioned earlier – and the specific orientation of organizations.

Due to general censorship in China, their government, specifically for sections concerned with Chinese regard, gives the limitation.

Another limit setting point is the topicality of the subject matter. This fact complicates the diversity as well as the kind of references. The search for up-to-date sources is restricted into websites and books, where books advance a more old-fashioned opinion and the internet a more modern one. This assimilates the resources according occurrence.

2. Product Communication

In this section of the thesis, the author explains and defines the scope of product communication. Where product communication is to be arranged in business sciences and
what affect it. Due to the importance of product communication, this section is an important part of this thesis to introduce the practical part of the thesis.

2.1. As Part of the Marketing Mix

Earlier Marketing was defined as sales promotion (Weiber, 1993, pp. 1-2). However, in
1960 McCarthy created the original Marketing Mix, which includes the so-called "4Ps".
This mix was giving the inaccurately described and defined marketing a shape (Fill,
2001, p. 25). The price is a very important part with the fastest impact on sales. In addition, visible on turnover figures. Of course, the product is key factor of marketing, because it affects not only the price, but also the place where to promote the product. You
would not place – which means distribute – a freezer in Antarctica.

Figure 1: 7P Marketing Mix (Own figure)

In 1981, Booms & Bitner created the claimed update of the marketing mix (Cambridge
Professional Academy Ltd, 2016). Augmented to the "classic" marketing mix – marked

red and blue in Figure 1 – whereas People, Processes and Physical Evidence – marked green in Figure 1.

Physical Evidence means that also every service, which usually is intangible, has a physical component. For example, a champagne as welcome-drink of a hotel's concierge.

A process is made of pieces. Connected one get a process-chain and these processes are part of the product or service. The service is done, when the product is delivered, additionally the delivery is a process the customers is paying for.

The people describe the employees. No matter if clerk, cleaning power or manager, everybody belongs to the company, is an important part and can influence the output (Cambridge Professional Academy Ltd, 2016).

The main topics for this thesis are the combination of the "2Ps" promotion – as the symbolic roof of communication – besides the product itself. These are marked red in above-mentioned Figure 1. As already said the product is the essential part of the marketing mix – no product, no marketing. However, the "P" which means products is not only the physical object or intangible service. Rather it includes the industry the product serves the segmented target group and is a significant part of determinants for price and corporate strategy.

2.2.   Pressure Triangle – Effectivity, Innovation, Costs

Innovation comes from the Latin word "innovatio", which means alteration, change or renewal. At the present time it is tantamount to R&D, creativity, ideas and new USPs and products. Indeed, innovation is not invention and can be more than that. In fact, there is no generally accepted definition; the only common attributes are the translated (Hoffmann, Lennerts, Schmitz, Stölzle, & Uebernickel, 2015, p. 397). In the thesis the focus is set on culture, product and communication, therefore the focus is set on technical innovations.

Firms' only incentive taken into account to innovate is profit (Rosenkranz, 1996). By investing – which creates cost, we will come to this part in the following passage – in ideas and new products the ulterior motive is to develop a new USP. An undiscovered

USP leads customers to buy; this brings higher revenue, due to the fact that it is a Unique Selling Proposition. This forces competitors to innovate themselves.

Costs are measureable. If it is labor, metal, oil, the rent for an office building or anything else. Everything is measureable autonomous of the currency. Nonetheless, due to the rapid trend in media since the 1990s (Hollensen, 2014, p. 484), especially in communication and IT – hardware and software – the demand for new products increase instantaneously. It is a strong driver and constraint, which the growing competition and velocity have on every organization. At the end, the investment will be represented in ratio to revenue, turnover, new customers or other KPIs. This brings us to the last passage in this section.

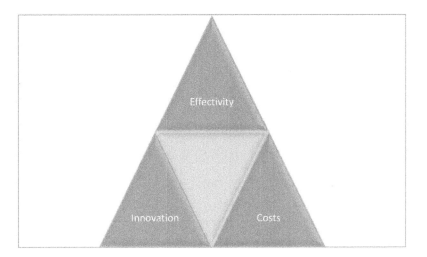

Figure 2: Pressure Triangle (Own Figure)

Effectivity – especially effective communication – is critical to any organization, but can help the organization (Hearst Newspaper, LLC, 2016). It can be misinterpreted; therefore, it has to be defined. The definition gives a concrete frame, in order to devise and measure what is a positive result and what is not. In addition, the definition prevents managers or executives of talking the results up, as the defined frame is set out in writing.

As observable in Figure 2, the mentioned parts build a pyramid that collapses like a house of cards if one part will not fit as necessary. The balance between costs, effectivity and innovation has to be weighed up carefully. So that the communication method follows valuable price-performance ratio.

3. Influences of cultural differences on product communication

To explain differences, the cultural characteristics have to be focused first. In the following passages, the author gives an impression of general difficulties global players face. Additionally, the countries China and India will be spotlighted in general facts, their culture and their economy.

3.1. General difficulties global acting companies have to face

Nowadays companies want to go global. Executives see that the domestic markets, where the product may be established, is or will be saturated on long-term view. To maximize their turnover, achieve higher reputation and at least grow, new markets should be discovered.

Henceforth the proven (core) strategy, which has been adapted to domestic needs, culture and target groups are known. As mentioned in chapter 1, other countries – respective their citizens and social groups – have other cultures and needs, the age patterns and ethnics may differentiate, as well as each other subgroup (Jandt, 1995).

But before the corporate growth can start executives have to decide whether to pursue a global or a multi-local – international – strategy with a variety of business areas (Gatignon & Kimberly, 2016). This decision influences following processes and decision. If the one focus an international strategy, the concentration is on some foreign markets. An example is Ikea, after the foundation in 1943 (IKEA Deutschland GmbH & Co. KG, 2016) Ikea opened the first subsidiary in another country in 1958 in Sweden. Moreover, went on in the Scandinavian area with subsidiaries in Norway (1963) and Denmark (1969). The first subsidiary outside of Scandinavia opened in 1973 in Switzerland, thirty years after the foundation (Schmid, 2006, p. 342).

Philip Kotler said, that 'all good marketing is local. Global companies know this and are going "glocal".' This means, those strategic conclusions, made by managements, by their competitiveness regarding the structure within an industry. In case of an industry of high-grade globalism, there are high interdependencies between extrinsic stakeholders: customers, suppliers and markets (Hollensen, 2014, pp. 22-24). A few large, powerful players (global) dominate the industry. Two good examples are producers of CPU, the most known and used in private PCs are Intel and AMD. The second is aircrafts; there the dominant players are Airbus and Boeing. Local business is more independent of other markets, due to the production of local products. A good example is "Kölsch" (Beer brewed in and 50 km surround Cologne), where either the ingredients can be generated by local firms or self-produced, if necessary.

Nevertheless, which industries can be globalized by which degree cannot be influenced by the firm, as it is mainly determined by the international marketing environment (Hollensen, 2014, pp. 24-25).

Significant and even more difficult in comparison to international strategies is the synchronized commercialization and sales all over the globe. A global player has no restriction in countries, continents or customers. Only the segmented target groups limit itself. To fit its target group(s), one has to divide carefully and even studies it (them). Social, cultural, historical, religious and every other thinkable arrangement in groups, as well as the markets the segmentation base on. Likewise, the high-paced development in media since the 1990s assign the companies new tasks, because that implicates compositions of new segments, target groups and even markets – a threat as well as an opportunity (Rohn, 2010, pp. 51-52).

By exploring a new market not only, the product is a key factor. For the reason that the foreign culture is comparatively unknown one has to analyze, plan and control all market applied company activities onto the declared market (Framson, 2007, pp. 24-25). This includes the entire Marketing Mix, due to possibly altered price conditions, ways of distribution; appreciation of communication (Apfelthaler, 1999).This is described roughly and shortened at the outset.

3.2.   China

The name China translated means middle kingdom. This is what Chinese think about their nation and how they see China in international comparison (Zinzius, 1996, p. 23). The People`s Republic of China has nearly 1.37 billion inhabitants, which makes it the most populous country in the world and the fourth biggest country in area with approximately 9.5 million square-kilometers (Statistisches Bundesamt, 2016). Two-thirds of the China's vast territory mountainous or desert and only one tenth is cultivated (Chow,

Holbert, Kelley, & Yu, 1997). These are some key facts that demonstrate the dimensions the country has in matters of population, size and the possibilities are attended by
these specifications.

To give an impression of the historical and political way until today, one starts in the
1970s – after the revolution in 1949. China concentrate on its own strengths and economists as well as policymakers recognized the necessity of overhauling the economic
system (Bell, et al., 1993). China had to be rejuvenating the economic system and began
to reform policies from 1978 to 1984, which let the trade fairs gain. Afterwards the es-
tablishment of the pricing system and the taxation has been reformed. Then, in the early
1990s, the socialist market system grew under the leading of Deng Xiaoping (Bell, et al.,
1993).

Nowadays China is confronted with stereotypes like communism, bad labor conditions
on the one hand and high-tech society and fast growing economy one the other hand.

3.2.1. Culture

Chinese culture has various facets, which are affected by diverse factors. Similar to other Asian countries Chinese focus on family, which sometimes includes the company as
well as the country. Personal connections are overwhelmingly important (Chow,
Holbert, Kelley, & Yu, 1997).

Figure 3: Cultural Dimensions of China according Hofstede (Own Figure)

This is also one aspect, which is considered in Geert Hofstede's cultural model. According the point Individualism in Figure 3, the index of 22 expresses a high value of group behavior, attesting the importance of personal connections. The six dimensions are generated to set a nation`s values in relation to others nation`s values. These ideals are influenced by their culture; hence, these dimensions declare the culture. However, they are researched within a group of one nation, thus they express a collective not an individual (Hofstede, Van Hofstede, & Minkov, 2010, pp. 28-30).

Following economists based on the work of Hofstede, Trompenaars and Hampden-Turner the dimensions have been filled with information and developed. In addition, the updated dimensions are geared to the origin dimensions created by Hofstede. Even more, Trompenaars and Hampden-Turner acknowledge the characteristics. Although the dimensions seen in Figure 4 are independent from the origin dimensions – alike Figure 3 – there are analogies. Even more, Trompenaars and Hampden Turner, accord Hofstede's research about cultural characteristics.

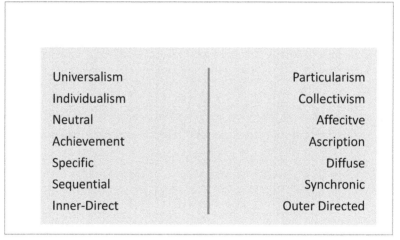

Universalism	Particularism
Individualism	Collectivism
Neutral	Affecitve
Achievement	Ascription
Specific	Diffuse
Sequential	Synchronic
Inner-Direct	Outer Directed

Figure 4: 7 Dimensions of Culture according Trompenaars & Hampden-Turner (Own Figure)

Important for business to concentrate on are specificity vs. diffuseness, inner-direct and outer direct based decisions and – as already mentioned according Hofstede and confirmed by Trompenaars and Hampden-Turner – individualism vs. collectivism. Chinese are, due to high collectivism value, interested in personal relations and ask direct and specific (Zinzius, 1996, pp. 45-47). But then again, they talk diffuse in business in order to be polite – according Confucianism – although they come to a pragmatic decision based on facts (Lang, 1998, pp. 29-32). Obviously, preparation affording one's requirements in order to avoid discrepancies is definitely recommended.

3.2.2. Market, Competitors, Demand

The Chinese market is segmented into four parts. Agricultural (Rural) Sector, Urban (Industrial) Sector and Service Sector are the classic sectors, but due to the strong influence and control of the government, an important "sector" consists of State-owned enterprises. This control built the strong industrial sector and modernized China, according the communists judgement.

After giving a short impression of Chinese markets, now the ICT industry and its characteristics including a specific view on the game consoles. That 10 companies out of 50 – this means 20% – most valuable Chinese brands are relocated in ICT sector expresses the competition within this industry. Moreover, 210,302 US$ millions of brand value of these Chinese ICT brands is an impressive number (Millward Brown, 2016). In comparison to these 10 brands Sony – with 34 US$ billions – and Microsoft – with 407 US$ billions – show the global role and importance of the two leaders of the industry (Forbes Media LLC, 2016).

An important point for companies producing and selling video game consoles has been the blanket restrictions – including manufacturing and selling consoles – which took effect in 2000. Due to governmental censors and possible adverse effects on Chinese youth, this ban enacted. After 15 years, the ban was lifted in 2014, as support for local industry and opening of the market (Tribune Publishing, 2016). This is comparable to a new market entry for

Based on half a billion gamers, the expectations have been tremendous. On the other hand, the lack of televisions, the high hardware cost and the – still prevailing – censorship for consoles and games, the short time trend is moderate. How the progress will remain to be seen.

3.3. India

Bharat Ganrajya – the Hindi term for Republic of India – places second with its 1.25 billion citizens in comparison to the world, only the population of China is higher. However, the area is only approximately a third with 3.3 million square-kilometers, which is number seven in comparison to world (Office of Public Affairs, 2016). India's dimensions are comparable to Chinas regarding size and inhabitants. Even in economy both are developing countries and have an average income below 10,000 US$ per year – China 7,572 US$ and India 1,608 US$ (Statistisches Bundesamt, 2016).

The Portuguese Vasco da Gama has been the first European who travelled around the African continent and discovered India in 1498, which made the Portuguese an important trading partner. Nevertheless, in 1600 Great Britain replaced Portugal as leading economic power and found the East India Company (iportale GmbH, 2016).

In 1947, India became independent of British-India and had a lot of changing political alliances after two periods of office by Indira Gandhi and her death in 1984. The present global economic crisis has strong influences on Indian economy, which let the Rupee decrease (Bundeszentrale für politische Bildung, 2016). Future will show how economy will develop and what milestones will be set.

3.3.1. Culture

Indian culture as well as Chinese – mentioned in chapter 3.2.1 – has many variations. Due to different ages and several registrations of tenures – Portuguese, British, Islamic, Persia – the culture developed richly colored like a flower. The more than 13 practiced religions – the main is Hindu with approximately 80% - point the variety up. Furthermore 100 languages of which 21 – besides English and Indian – are registered as official languages, which is another indicator for cultural diversity (Deutsche Zentrale für Tourismus e.V., 2016; Dalmia & Sadana, 2012, pp. XIV-XVII).

In business, Indians have diverse attitudes too, due to the variety of religions, ethnic groups and languages. According same religious orientation there will be commonalities, the way business is done in India. Indians search for guides and thinkers, gurus, they can trust in look up to. Indian businesspersons want to gain the boss' favor; this explains the high PDI of 77 according Hofstede's cultural dimensions in Figure 5. Even though, if they are not lucky with their boss or even with their forecast career prospects, other options will be taken into consideration (Rodewald, 2007, p. 66). Thus describes the relatively small UAI of 40 in Figure 5, which means that Indians do not avoid risks.

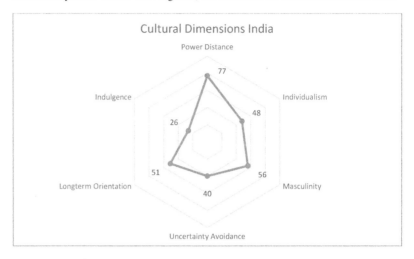

Figure 5: Cultural Dimensions of India according Hofstede (Own Figure)

According their caste consciousness Indians index for individualism according Hofstede is 48 (Figure 5). Neither it is a high value nor is it a low one, as they stay together in a collective within one caste, whereas they are individual in the face of other people. Apart from the relatively low value of masculinity (56 in Figure 5), the women still expected to be submissive or obedient. However, these are continuous self-developing values determined by humans and of humans (Pawan S., 2010).

At the end of this passage the key is, to prepare oneself for provoking cultural mistakes, a lot of prearrangement is necessary. Whether it is India or – mentioned in section 3.2.1 – China.

3.3.2. Market, Competitors, Demand

A high percentage of 72% lived a rural life in 2001 according the census, where nowadays more and more young Indians move to bigger cities to work. The juvenescence makes India, as well as China with an average of 8.73%, a powerful economy with average growth of GDP of 7.18% including future predictions. This comparison, shown in Figure 6, makes the immense power clear by exposing the limitations for a global economy, as Germany is (StatisticsTimes.com, 2016).

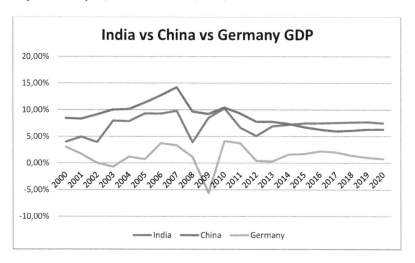

Figure 6: GDPs of India, China, and Germany from 2000-2020 (Own figure, data by StatisticsTimes.com, 2016)

In contrast to the economic growth, the primary sector is still the main one in India. On the one hand, this sector contributes almost 17% of the GDP, whereas approximately 52.1% – more the 600 million people – work in this sector. The problem will be that this sector is dependent on natural resources, which are dependent on weather, air and other not susceptible circumstances.

The second sector – producing and manufacturing – has a share of 30% of the GDP by 2014. The third sector – service sector – is the most powerful sector with 53% share of the GDP (Statista GmbH, 2016). These high measurements are result of an adjustment and the loss of around 30% of agriculture since 1960/61 (Chopra, et al., 1995, p. 5).

One of the biggest economic drivers is and will be the Software-IT-Industry. For the reason that the US economy declined and many jobs of the back office moved to India, there is a lot of enthusiasm and optimism. To express the scale: only in Bangalore live nearly 500,000 IT workers alongside 7 million citizens. Another point is the growth of 9% per year (Deresky, 2014, p. 111).

This IT-Sector includes the topic of electronic consumer products – specifically Smartphones in India. Although 22% - equates 275 million people or at least thrice Germany – live beyond the poverty line and 5% (62.5 million) are analphabets (Handelsblatt GmbH, 2016), India just crossed the mark of 1 billion mobile subscribers. However, by now only 30% are using smartphones, the next wave will be the update to smartphones (Forbes Media LLC, 2016; Statista GmbH, 2016).

The potential for a global economic power is given, by growth, landscape, workface and technological knowledge, future will show if the former developing country is able to compound these facts and implement them to become a developed and economical powerful country.

4. Case Example of Intercultural Product Communication

This section of the thesis makes an example of cultural communication for subsequent following products of the organizations Sony, Microsoft, Samsung and Apple. At the beginning the organizations will be surveyed, before whose core strategy will be explained.

Afterwards the author examines how strong the different core strategies are transferred and implemented to the products: Sony strategy to PS4, Microsoft strategy to Xbox One, Samsung strategy to Samsung Galaxy S6 Edge+ and Apple strategy to IPhone 6S Plus.

The last part of each product passage evaluates, if there are discrepancies within the product communication in the specific country and the corresponding core strategy, due to cultural backgrounds.

4.1. Sony

The Japanese company entered the market in May 1946, founded by Masaru Ibuka and Akio Morita, initially called Tokyo Tsushin Kogyo (Tokyo Telecommunications Engineering Corporation or TTK) (Ohga, 2008, p. 1).

Their first product was not a Walkman, a flat screen TV or any other high-tech product, but a rice cooker. It failed commercially. Twelve years later, in 1958, the founders renamed the company into SONY adapted from the Latin word 'sonus', which means 'sound' (News Limited, 2016).

Even before the new name was known, transistor radios were invented, which made a profit and consequently had to be manufactured in mass production. However, in 1964 the first successful milestone was set with the Trinitron television, which entered the market during an inauspicious time. Color televisions have been sold since the fifties. The advantage of the pioneers as well as high producing costs made the market entry a gamble. The new format technique makes the picture clearer and brighter than before. These product innovations made the Trinitron a phenomenal success (Ohga, 2008, pp. 32-34; Troester, 2016).

Another important pillar Sony established during the joint venture with CBS was cultivating singers. The movie 'The Graduate' and attendant CBS release of 'The sound of

Silence' by Simon and Garfunkel supported the incoming orders as well as the progress of signing prominent recording stars (Ohga, 2008, pp. 56-57).

One of the biggest and most important Innovations was the Walkman in 1979. The Walkman with all it various lines and designs has been retired in 2010 with over 400 million sold devices, 200 of them cassette players (Vox Media, 2016).

Nowadays Sony is known for almost every consumer electronic hardware product. Blu-Ray or DVD players, 4K-Televisions, MP4-Player, mobile phones, movies and of course game consoles, whereon the author focus on in the next passage and the next chapters.

The Sony PlayStation would not exist without Nintendo's inadvertent assistance. Nintendo wanted a CD-Drive to be created by Sony; however, Phillips awarded the funding. So Sony entered the game console PlayStation (PS one or PSX) itself in 1994. With their followers PlayStation2 in 2000, PlayStation3 in 2006 and the current device PlayStation4 in 2013 the game consoles have been approved continuously (Savoya Consulting UG, 2016) and the competition gets harder with Microsoft's Xbox One, which will be mentioned in chapter 4.2 the author sets the detailed focus on the PlayStation in chapter 4.1.2 to survey the specifications.

4.1.1. Core Strategy

Sony incarnates the mission of a company to raise and satisfy the customer's curiosity. With passion for technology, design, contents and services compared with the pursuit for innovations. A company's core strategy can often be linked to its core competency. The original core competency of Sony is to miniaturize its products, that is the technical knowledge. As it is visible through radios, transistors, camcorders, portable game consoles and the Walkman (White, 2004, pp. 683-684).

Sony, under Morita, was far ahead of its time by going for 'glocalization' in the early sixties. This means there have been subsidiaries all over the globe, but the managers have been locally sensitive according the specific needs and characteristics of their own markets (Nathan, 2001, p. 289). This makes Sony as much insiders as local companies and still able to enjoy the benefits of global scale operations. The result is a multinational company (MNC) or a multi-domestic company (MDC). This a specific form of globalization by focusing on foreign characteristics and not using one strategy for the whole world.

Even corporate identity carries the strategy. Through communication, behavior and symbolism it emerges. All three points may be experienced internal and external. To focus on external factors, the author starts with the brand and the logo, which belongs to communication and symbolism. Due to the monolithic identity structure and the specific writing of Sony all products carry the same corporate name, produces strong value of brand recognition (Cornelissen, 2004, pp. 72-73). The design of the hardware is according Norio Ogha, former CEO of Sony Corp, against early wooden cases. It shall be simple, clear, and made of grey or black material – metal or metal look.

The author concludes that Sony's core competency has only been an initial ignition for the company. Globally products of Sony are seen as high quality, miniaturized customer electronics, whereon no switch is inconsiderately and the shape as well as the design is recognizable overall. Sony does not invent new products, but rather innovate, improve and miniaturize an established product. The core strategy can be defined as 'glocal' improvement and miniaturization – the competitive advantage – of technology, while giving the specific simple, but smart Sony design and functionality.

4.1.2. Implementation on PlayStation 4

Sony's PlayStation 4 is the company's newest generation of game console and follow in PS3's and even more PS2's big footsteps, as the most sold game consoles worldwide.

Sony Corp's core strategy to miniaturize and improve already existing hardware devices, is not completely compatible to PS4's. As game consoles need sufficient space for the data medium, Blu-Ray in this case, miniaturizing comparable to competitors is not possible. Still, improving in comparison to elder models is one of the keys of the Sony Interactive – Sony Corp subsidiary enterprise – strategy. Apart from former strategies, of PS3 and PS2, to strengthen and merchandise the particular data medium – DVD or rather Blu-Ray – the company focuses on their core business. This is the result of the competition between the Blu-Ray, which should substitute the DVD and the HD-DVD as primary home video format, the DVD is still in usage (Bidness ETC, 2016). Furthermore, with their position in home and cinema entertainment Sony merchandises especially its video and music applications usable with the PS4, which correlate with current customer's network needs according the PlayStation E3 Press Conference 2013 (PlayStation, 2016).

The implementation of Sony Corp's core strategy is, as mentioned, not completely compatible. Summing up, the transfer of parts of the core strategy such as improvement of existing technologies and the considerate, simple, sharp and smart design in lusterless black draws conclusions from the origin of the PlayStation 4. This implicates a high recognition of the brand, due to design and attributes.

4.1.3. Cultural Characteristics of Product Communication on Chinese Market

For the purpose of this chapter of the thesis, the author verifies, if the global core strategy of Sony Corp, which is already adjusted for game consoles due to specific circumstances such as necessary space for hardware, is accomplished in China or has been adapted, because of explicit cultural characteristics.

Sony could sell PS4 devices since 2013 worldwide, meanwhile in China young adults switched to gaming via computers and mobile devices, due to the governmental ban, imposed in 2000. The prohibition was lifted in 2014, which is in immense disadvantage. Relating to the fact that also the parent models PS2 and PS3 had no chance to compete mentioned gaming services. The new release in March 2015 has been comparable to a completely new market entry, against competitors with 15 years advanced knowledge about the general and the gamers' culture. Other facts influencing the product communication in China is the relatively high price of 2,899 yuan ($467) and the tough censorship, which limits the portfolio of games according governmental guidelines, for example: no glorification of drugs or violence (Thomson Reuters, 2016).

Due to these tough restrictions the ambitions have not been reached. The more than 500 million gamers bought approximately half a million legal PS4 and Xbox One gaming consoles combined. This cannot be what Sony expected and even an estimated import of grey market consoles of 1.5 million gaming consoles would be a considerably low number regarding to a population of more than 1.3 billion. Other challenges are the high price relating to a relatively low average income and that there do not exist any Chinese made games for Chinese. It means, that most games – which are allowed according the censorship – are made by developers all over the world, but most content is made for western culture (ZhugeEx, ZhugeEx Blog, 2016). Two examples are Call of Duty (COD) and GTA V; both are figureheads of gaming consoles. Firstly, both games are not allowed due to the censorship, due to glorification of violence, drugs, alcohol and sex. Secondly, COD plays in Europe and USA, and GTA in two fictitious cities Los Santos – based on Los Angeles – and Los Santos – based on San Andreas. No allowance and no cultural adaption.

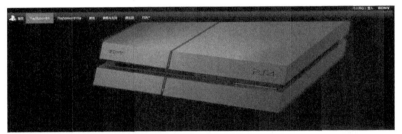

Figure 7: PlayStation US-Website (Sony Interactive Entertainment LLC, 2016)

Figure 8: PlayStation China Website (Sony Interactive Entertainment LLC, 2016)

In addition, the cultural adaption within the several web presences has only small differences. The modifications seem to have cultural and governmental reasons. While the American website in Figure 7 is colorful and in the background, a video is running, the Chinese website in Figure 8 is completely black. Strict censorship guidelines regarding the video that runs can be a cause. Other pages, for example the German or the Italian website, do not even show the device. However, in Europe the market is approximately matured and the device well known. The second small disparity is the lighting PS4 in China and the standing one in the US. Possibly a cultural reason which refers to Chinese who are in general not tall and take a bow to welcome someone, while the Americans stand stereotypical for big entrances, the bigger the better. Americans love the show.

Nevertheless, the company seems to be interested in winning market share, no matter who will buy the PS4. The first entirely in China made game 'Koi' (Fingas, 2016) is released in April 2016, which is meant to hit the Chinese culture and appeal not only to young adults – focus group – but also to older game console interested people. This mirrors in the first advertising for China released in March 2016 – one year after the market entry – where children, young adults and elderly people play together with the gaming console. It reflects the cultural characteristics, which express the importance of family and personal connections for Chinese, like mentioned in chapter 3.2.1. and Hofstede`s dimension individualism (see Figure 3), which is very low with 22. Furthermore, it is a contrast to general commercials of gaming consoles, wherein action sequences are an essential part to catch the gamers' attention. Additionally, they play classic and cultic games. These games are partial focused on Asian culture like Street Fighter – obviously allowed – where most fighters are Asian, although violence is glorified, Ridge Racer and Final Fantasy (ZhugeEx, YouTube, 2016).

Concluding the author observes an increasing cultural consideration of the Chinese market. At the beginning the effort, has not been sufficient, which leads back to the hindered market entrance, the strict censorship and highly competitive market. Possibly, at the beginning, the importance of cultural adaption has been underrated and the chances to gain high market shares have not been evaluated correctly. However, later Sony realizes the vast potential due to the high an increasing population. The circumstance for the present will not change and if Sony is willing to win market share, will be shown. However, the organization definitely has to invest in cultural adapted communication and development concerning games; otherwise, it will be a tough business venture.

4.2.   Microsoft

Almost everybody knows the American organization Microsoft as one of the world biggest and most known companies. Already in 1995, 140 million out of 170 million PC in private usage, which equals to more than 80%, were used under an operating system made by Microsoft (Cusumano & Selby, 1996, p. 13).

In 1975, Bill Gates and Paul Allen decided to start their own company, called Micro-Soft the hyphen dropped a few months later. However, the both computer hobbyists met each other in 1967, at Lakeside School. In this school, he had the possibility to use a simple teletypewriter, which was expensive. Bill Gates learned the programming language BASIC and together with Paul Allen, he earned his first money by testing computer programs. As collective, both electronic experts found their first business Traf-O-Data in 1972, for traffic count systems and traffic lead systems (Cusumano & Selby, 1996, pp. 26-28).

Their first and most important big coup was the request of IBM to configure its PCs with MS-DOS as operating system in 1981. MS-DOS and Windows are probably Microsoft's best-known products (Musolf, 2008, pp. 6-14). After this deal, the company grew continuous and the organizational structure had to be adapted synchronous to the growth – otherwise the company could not keep pace with it. A free working unit business works for small projects and start-ups, but not for a growing up software enterprise like Microsoft begun to become. During the development of the organizational, structure important milestones occurred. The first milestone in 1984 was the disposition of separate focus groups for each department as well as the setting of expert functions in addition to the focus groups. Then, in 1986, the beginning of Post-mortem reports started, wherein problems and solution statements were documented. The change of Mike Maples in 1988, who arranged smaller business units, from IBM to Microsoft was another important step, before in 1992 he – Executive Vice President – led the World Wide Product Group under which the system and the applications sector were centralized. In the same year, the Office of the President was created. In 1993, the marketing teams on level of divisions were centralized and the business units were renamed into product units with the effect of a revolution of orientation, collaboration and solution identification (Cusumano & Selby, 1996, pp. 35-45). This is not the end of change or milestones, because Microsoft is a company without standstill.

Established as platform leader in personal computers and bolstered up with a heavy billion revenue, Microsoft recognized the profit of Nintendo and of course Sony in the
game console market. Due to the providing of Windows CE for SEGA and the involving information Microsoft could collect, the distance was not too far. In 2001, the Xbox
was presented in America, but rather 2002 in Europe and Japan. The launch was tough
due to years of advantages of their competitors and already in 2003 Microsoft begun
planning the next generation of gaming console (Marshall, 2016). In chapter 4.2.2, the
author observes the current-gen gaming console of Microsoft – Xbox One – closer.

4.2.1. Core Strategy

What are values exactly? 'Value' is a term of orientation and/or belief people within a
social group – also at workplace – comply with. Microsoft refers to values or its core
strategy as mission. The mission: every household and every desk shall have its own
personal computer.

The software industry is highly competitive due to a multitude of suppliers for each
program, task or application. This is why the competitive advantage of Microsoft – as
one of the Pioneers in computer industry – tries to dominate the market by using its ad-
vances. To reach the high value of competitive advantage, following points are important drivers.

These points have an immense influence on the core strategy of Microsoft. Focus young
mass markets and create industrial standards with good products, therefore most initial
offerings of Microsoft are not industry leaders, but through continuous improvement
achieve the status of industrial and private standard. That happened with MS-DOS,
Windows 95, Word and other office systems (Cushman & Sanderson King, 2001, pp.
36-38).

Another point supporting Microsoft applications and operating systems considered as
standard are exclusive agreements for MS-DOS and Windows such as Intel with micro-
processors. Those contracts let Microsoft have a second benefit, besides the consideration as standard; they generate continuous profit without sales costs due to long-term
obligation (Cusumano & Selby, 1996, pp. 106-107). To compete in this industry, the
company invests hundreds of millions year in and year out for R&D, which neither eve-

ry competitor nor a start-up can afford (Cusumano & Selby, 1996, pp. 120-122). Likewise supporting the standard, the peripheral equipment act as consolidation for established products. This equipment was only usable with one specific operating system. 'Was' because nowadays the peripheral equipment is usable overall operating systems due to wireless usage or downloaded installations according the own operating system.

The final and most visionary point – looking into the future already in past – is product integration in two ways. Firstly, specific customer need and wishes – for example desktop clocks, organizer, calendars, calculator, screen saver or other small applications – which are integrated for private households by Microsoft itself.

Secondly, under the market power of Microsoft purchasing employees and even smaller firms – so knowledge – is not too difficult. Imagine you develop an explicit program with vast potential for privates and business, usable on computers. You get a call of Microsoft in order to configure their operating system with your program. If you do not go to the appointment, you will be excluded. Millions of personal computers without your program. Your dream is almost gone. This is business and a powerful enterprise like Microsoft has these possibilities.

At the end of this section, the core strategy of Microsoft can be concluded. The company tries to gain the technology by being part of for it necessary alliances to set standards for applications used on even standard operating systems. Microsoft wants to develop products acting as standard on the specific interface. Furthermore, it mimics technologies and improve them for own products and aims. Microsoft core competency is creating and developing software and dominating the market, with an uncatchable market share.

4.2.2. Implementation on Xbox One

Gaming consoles were not the key or flagship product from Microsoft and with entering
the market in March 2000 with the Xbox follower in comparison to the industry leaders
PlayStation (1994) and Nintendo (1983) or Sega Mega Drive (1988). Microsoft recognized the gains the mentioned companies bring in and its success with the creation of
DirectX, a set of application programming interfaces (APIs), and the company decided
in 1998 to produce its own gaming console. In addition, the name was given the APIs as
it was called DirectX Box at the beginning, before market testing gives a hint in this
direction (Griffith, 2016).

The transfer of Microsoft's core strategy onto the Xbox product line was quite difficile,
because although the budget was available and the software was a problem neither, the
company had no experience at all in this industry. In addition, the focus was set on
software not on hardware. Therefore, Microsoft took advantage of Bungie Studios – a
necessary alliance – who developed Halo. Until today the best-known and most sold
Xbox, this contributes a massive part to the increasing acceptance of the Microsoft
Xbox.

Microsoft used and still uses the same abilities in the development of the Xbox as in
developing software: innovate and/or improve techniques for own products. Two examples are Kinect – the body movement recognizer. With Kinect, the gamers can play with
their own bodies, recorded by cameras and sensors. Secondly the Xbox was the first
gaming console with a hard drive and able to rip audio CDs. Microsoft rapidly adopts
and implement the customer's wishes e.g. a slim and therefore economic device or Wi-
Fi.

All these skills were used to lift the Xbox One to the strongest competitor of Sony's
PlayStation 4. Besides the necessity to pay Sony for the Blu-Ray technology, Microsoft
configure its current-gen gaming console with a lot of own services such as Skype or its
exclusive titles like Halo 5 or Dead Rising 3.

The core strategy has almost been perfectly implemented onto the Xbox One, where
possible. Concluded: necessary alliances were built, innovations were created, invest-
ments were activated, customer wishes and needs were identified and satisfied and the
own development goes on. Dominating this industry with an uncatchable market share
is the only point, which is not transferred. Due to the late industry and market entry Mi-

crosoft took the role of the follower and not the pioneer. Nevertheless, Microsoft come up to the market leader PlayStation, due to constructive realization of the own core competencies.

4.2.3. Cultural Characteristics of Product Communication on Chinese Market

Microsoft competes in China politically with the same resistance as Sony does. The governmental ban on the production as well as the sale of game consoles has its effects even there. Microsoft did not wait too long introducing the Xbox One in China, so that the Xbox One was the first official foreign game console, which was introduced after the ban, by end of September 2014 and therefore half a year before the PlayStation 4. The distinct computer and mobile gaming culture pressurizes Microsoft, so that the earlier entry into the Chinese market probably secures a better starting position against Sony's PlayStation.

The Xbox seems to have been better prepared concerning the cultural circumstances, entering inclusive a locally developed game – 'Naughty Kitties' – that shall appeal the stereotypical infatuation of Asians in cats. In BesTV, also a local partner has already been found. Nevertheless, the cutting of the blockbuster titles like 'Halo' or 'Titanfall' are readable within the sales figures related to the restrained start (Mendoza, 2016).

Microsoft's first commercial for the Chinese version of the Xbox One, shown on the E3 fair in 2013, mirrors every prejudice the western world has against Chinese. The video advertisement shows a high school student coming home, while the mother is watching a video on the Xbox One, but pausing by voice command to greet the son. Then the son wants to play 'Forza 5', when the mother is leading him to handle several tasks, from homework for school, learning English, doing Mathematics and downloading a new learning app. At the end, the son is allowed to play for a while, due to having done all tasks (Youku, 2016). Obviously, on the one hand, this video shall express the diversity of the Xbox One, but on the other hand, this lead the viewer to be confirmed in stereotypes, such as discipline, tough work, multi-tasking and getting drilled. Which view predominates is not clear.

In another clip, only short game teasers are shown wherein no specific cultural adaption is observable, besides a Chinese game. Nevertheless, not allowed games according the censorship are visible too (Jou, 2016). The route is not yet clear and has to be improved.

Where in videos Microsoft adapt cultural characteristics in parts the compared websites are identical as comparable in Figure 9, where the Chinese page is on the top and the US page is below. This shows that the strategy is not coherently adapted to China as new and cultural different market.

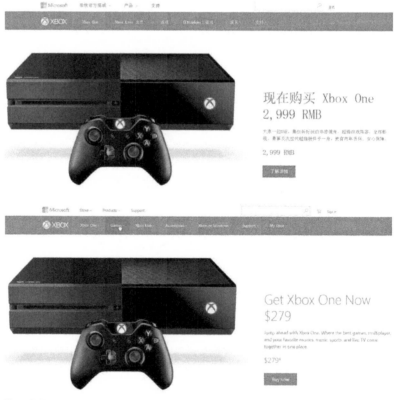

Figure 9: Comparison of US and Chinese Xbox Websites (Microsoft Corp, 2016; Microsoft Corp, 2016)

Microsoft – like Sony PlayStation too – has to face up the competition with Chinese industry leader, computer and mobile devices. Due to years collecting information about the culture – specifically the gaming culture – there is lot of work. However, Microsoft immediately recognized the huge potential of the country and the number of potential customers.

4.3. Samsung

The Samsung Group by far is the biggest conglomerate in South Korea and employs
nearly half a million people all over the globe. 'Samsung' in Korean means 'three stars',
the name was chosen because the company wants to shine bright like powerful Asian
conglomerates – also called 'Jaebol' in Korea, which means big family enterprise – like
Mitsubishi – in Japanese 'three stars', too – and Mitsui – 'three founts'. Lee Byung
Chull founded the company in 1938 in Daegu, Korea. In 1951, Samsung Moolson established – now Samsung Corporation (Samsung, 2016).

Even in the earlier years of the company, the built of the conglomerate began by buying
several companies in 1954 Ankuk Fire & Marine Insurance – renamed in Samsung Fire
& Marine Insurance – and 1963 DongBang Life Insurance – renamed in Samsung Life
Insurance. This point out that Samsung did not restrict itself into consumer electronics.
Additionally, the organization found more and more affiliated companies such as Cheil
Industries Inc. in 1954, Joong-Ang Development (nowadays known as Samsung Ever-
land) in 1966 or Samsung-Sanyo Electronics, which was renamed in March 1975 into
Samsung Electro-Mechanics and merged in March 1977 with Samsung Electronics
(Samsung, 2016).

During the 1970ies, the production of consumer electronic products increased sharply.
Already in 1976 Samsung produced the millionth black-and-white television and in
1978 the four millionth and in 1989 the 20 millionth. Followed by washing machines,
microwaves, air conditioning systems, PCs, camcorders, semiconductor products, mobile phones and many more.

This superiority offers even more: one of the biggest dockyards worldwide – under
Samsung Heavy Industries – as well as one of the biggest life insurance – the Samsung
Life Insurance – and even hospitals, construction firms, hotels, chemical plants and
even more. A variation of companies of all industries under one big conglomerate
(Rohwetter, 2012). On the other hand, this power pressurizes the whole market and almost every competitor. In addition, even government such as Germany's keep the
strength and power in view, due to possible dishonest market advantages. This power is
also a consequence of not outsourcing the production, in this way Samsung is an important supplier for its competitors especially Apple. Not only displays for the iPhones,
iPads and the iWatch, but particularly the processor of the A9 processor – the heart of

every electronic product – is approximately by 80% made by Samsung (9to5mac.com, 2016).

The story of Samsung mobile phones started in 1991 with the development of first mobile handset. Eight years later the first wireless internet phone has been developed – nowadays Smartphone. The trend became faster from year to year, 2002 the first mobile phone with 65,000 colors and in 2004 already sold 20,000,000 mobile phones in the US. In 2010, the flagship mobile phone line Galaxy S launched. Since 2012 Samsung is the world's largest mobile phone make and in September 2016 the Galaxy S6 edge+ has been released (Samsung, 2016; Siebenhaar, 2016).

In the next chapter the author focus on the core strategy and then goes on to the realization and implementation of this strategy for the smartphone Samsung Galaxy S6 edge+, before he concerns himself with the cultural characteristics of the product communication in India.

4.3.1. Core Strategy

A core strategy in general is not that difficult to filter it out, but in the case of Samsung, one has to look through the quantity and diversity of sub companies of many industries.

Core pillars of Samsung's strategy are firstly, learning from competitors as a fast follower and until today no pioneer. The company learns rapidly and transfers the technique ad-hoc on its own products and update the technique and product according market and customer needs. Secondly, no fails are tolerated and this pressure is exerted within the whole organization. Therefore, the own production plants are enormously important; they give Samsung the opportunity to make and enforce quick decisions, due to strength hierarchies (Nisen, 2016).

Samsung understands the importance of consumers and orient its innovations on their needs and wishes. Combined with smart and well-designed products it is a central topic of the core strategy, too. Samsung goes further by not designing for uniqueness, but also for interacting with users and reflecting them. Three more factors are focus on marketing, focus on quality and focus on innovations. With Apple and Google, Samsung is one of the largest investor in R&D and has more than 20 research and development centers across the world. Through alliances, partnerships, and rapid development, the company keeps itself abreast of latest technologies. By beginning of the 90s, Samsung sponsored some of the biggest sporting events across all the games, which encouraged the brand awareness. The third point – quality – appears as supplier. By supplying its competitors, the quality speaks in its favor; otherwise, they would not buy these components (M., Vembu, Agarwal, Dubey, & Kalkotwar, 2013, pp. 189-191).

Samsung has a tricky core strategy, its core competence is learning by competitors and implementing in own products. Due to market appearance overall industries, the company can work with synergies, which expresses in the comparative advantage and the fast following strategy. Everybody in this company wants to be number one in every industry – they have the will. Samsung enforces itself by its organizational structure, which is leaded by a big family.

4.3.2. Implementation on Galaxy S6 Edge+

Not learning by competitors or the market is impossible. The author can say the core strategy has been implemented perfectly, done. Now it has to be illustrated in detail. The first Samsung Galaxy S launched in 2010 and until today, this product line is the flagship series. As the Samsung started the line 3 years after Apple launched its first iPhone edition, obviously the Galaxy S line is the follower, like the company's core strategy concept itself, too.

The current-gen flagship model transcends the core strategy of adapting competitors' innovations and copy them. Although lot of components of the Galaxy S6 Edge+ are not reinvented, like the rounded corners, the fingerprint sensor or the menu navigation, but the rounded down edges are an invention and are distinctive brand recognition features of the newest editions of Galaxy Smartphones.

Visually the line has developed in size and performance, due to technical enhancements, similar to Apple's iPhone. However, the general optic as well as the haptic did not change, so that the recognition of the Galaxy S line smartphones is high.

To give a résumé the implementation and transfer of the core strategy is succeeded technical and optical as well. Learn, transfer and improve of competitors' experiences for own purposes has been realized completely.

4.3.3. Cultural Characteristics of Product Communication on Indian Market

Researching the cultural adaption of smartphones is very difficult, because a smartphone is a multi-purpose product and does almost everything. Therefore, an adaption of the product itself is not necessary. All the more important is: what do Indians the smartphones use for? What needs and wishes do they have? Moreover, is the communication B2C oriented this way? In this section, the author shows with examples and connection to mentioned models in what way these questions can be answered.

The Indian smartphone market is highly competitive, both low-priced vendors like Intex or Micromax Informatics, as well as the top models of the global players like Samsung, Apple, HTC and Sony want to gain their market shares of over 1 billion potential customers and by the end of 2015 nearly 170 million smartphone users. Samsung as the market leader in India with 25 % market share wants secure its position and therefore client's interests must be known exactly (Times Internet Limited, 2016).

Figure 10: Indian Samsung Website (Samsung Corp, 2016)

Indians are less brand-oriented; they scrutinize price and features, so they prefer a smartphone with good price-performance ratio. Specifically, the working memory, the camera and the LTE technology in combination with a low cost are key points in the search for the perfect smartphone in India (Abhishek, 2016). This makes the competitiveness in terms of costs difficult for Samsung.

Thus, the features must be communicated in a better way to potential consumers. Samsung does not concern this cultural specificity. Firstly, the websites are equal and country independently created: unfussy, through the company-specific blue something cool and pragmatic, well to observe and simple enumerated facts like observable in Figure10. This is suitable for the already as factual described Indians. The video commercials are not emotional, but show subjectively in a beautiful way the features of the Samsung Galaxy S6 Edge +. It is especially the USP – the rounded edges – that are focused (Samsung Mobile, 2016) .

Whether this minimalist and general commercialization will be received in a long-term view on the Indian market remains above all to be seen with a view of the comparatively high costs. Since the Indian average income cannot be compared with an American or a European.

4.4. Apple

Apple started in 1976. The young electronic nerds Steven Paul Jobs, Stephen Wozniak and Ron Gerald Wayne are the entrepreneurs who founded the enterprise. They began by making personal computers. Already in 1983, the company approached $1 billion, which obviously needed to organizational results due to continuous growth.

First of April 1976, Los Altos, California: next to San Francisco – an area, which is called Silicon Valley, due to its concentrated computer and semiconductor industry – the company was founded in the parental home of Steve Jobs. With the Apple I, they had their first success. On the way of this success, also the distinctive Logo occurred. Apple sold 50 pieces to 'Byte Shop', a local electronic shop. The shop advertised with:"Byte in an Apple", from then on the logo was the bitten Apple (Erdmann, 2011, pp. 18-19:31-33). Already one year later in 1977, Apple made its breakthrough with the Apple II. In this fiscal year, Apple had a turnover of 800,000 Dollar and another year later the decuple. Both the IPO stock price of 22 Dollar in 1980 and the rise to round about 90 Dollar today (OnVista Group, 2016) and temporary highs about 400 Dollar is a lead for its success.

In 1983, Apple showed its affinity for a perfect stage-managed advertisement. With an epic TV-Spot, this dramatically makes the philosophy and the will to be different clear. The 30 seconds spot is based on George Orwell's Vision of 1984 and even called '1984'. An athletic woman runs – hunted by a kind of security or army – with a Hammer in her hands through a big screen. The screen shows the leader, who talks to a mass of similar closed grey, will-less and viewless people. The leader's words reveal conformity, one will one people – in short no individuality. The woman throws the hammer into the screen and the slogan fade in: "On January 24th, Apple Computers will introduce Mac-intosh. And you'll see why 1984 won't be like '1984'." The advertisement was a hint for future spots and only on YouTube, more than 10.5 million people watched it (Erdmann, 2011, pp. 43-45).

In September 1985, Steve Jobs has been resigned and sold 1 million of his Apple shares, so that from then on John Sculley had exclusively power. Differently than maybe thought, the visions of Apple and the innovations plant did not stop. In the following years, the focus seemed to move to smaller and mobile handhelds. The project 'Newton' from 1987 until the completion in 1993 is a good example for the new way of consumer electronics. However, the competitors did not remain static, neither regarding PDAs, nor desktop PCs. The computer and software industry got highly competitive; Microsoft and IBM enlarged their marked shares.

During the solo project of Steve Jobs, with 'NeXT', it seemed as if Apple were losing its identity, because he stood for individualism, creativity and lifestyle, like no other and is deemed to be the 'iGod'. Moreover, 12 years after his notice Apple's acquisition of NeXT, Steve Jobs was back, but at the beginning as consultant. Before – in 1997 – he became interim CEO and two and a half years later official (Gartz, 2005, pp. 228-231). This happened because of the problems with the operating system and the crisis of Apple.

The resurgence began in 1997 with a $150 million investment of Microsoft in shares of Apple and an agreement, which allowed both companies to get the others products licensed. From a product-specific point of view, the savior was the iMac with the completely new blue colored case. In addition, the most influential person during the resurgence of Apple was the principal designer of the iMac, iPod, iBook and iPhone, Jonathan Ive. From then on Apple pulled one of the biggest turnarounds in business history (O'Grady, 2009, pp. 11-14).

The topic iPhone and its development will be focused in 4.2.2., as well as the implementation of Apple's strategy on this product.

4.4.1. Core Strategy

One sentence focus on the rivalry against Microsoft and on a corporate identity characteristic of Apple:

> "The only problem with Microsoft is they just have no taste. They have absolutely no taste. And I don't mean that in a small way, I mean that in a big way, in the sense that they don't think of original ideas, and they don't bring much culture into their products." Steve Jobs.

Apple wants to be different, that is a main topic in its strategy, combined with 'taste'. Nevertheless, what strategic points exactly made Apple become one of the leading IT enterprises? The author analyses exact characteristics, which specify the keys to the core strategy of Apple and how the company transfers it into other countries and cultures.

The mentioned point '*taste*' is meant to be a key. From the beginning Steve Jobs – former CEO – disliked the standard visual appearance of computers – quadratic, black, plastically and everyone looks like the other. He seemed to be obsessed of design and look. Even the size has to fit. Once he showed up with a telephone directory in a meeting, he threw it on the table and said:" This size the Macintosh can be. If it is bigger, it will not succeed." He stimulates the customer's emotion by having an emotional relationship to electronic devices made by Apple (Wala, 2011, pp. 65-68).

Apple core competency is the ability to make technology easy and usable. According to customer needs not be in need of an explanation. This consumer friendly design began with the launch of the Apple Macintosh in 1984, which were sold immediately, although it was a premium-price product. However, exactly this is another strategic factor of Apple (Thompson, 2001, pp. 554-557).

An additional significant point for the success is producing and especially distributing new innovative products, so called core products. At the beginning of the 21st century, Apple had to renew its strategy from a one-product strategy – the Apple Macintosh – to innovate new products. The era of the "i" began and started in 1998 with the iMac, but the iPod 1st Generation in 2001 followed by several generations of iPods, iMacs, iBooks, iTunes and one of the strongest Apple products in 2007 the iPhone. Apple renewed the music market and the mobile phone market with its innovative products and – by the way – managed a turnaround (de Wit & Meyer, 2010, pp. 685-689).

Owing to mentioned statements, Apple's strategy can be summarized as follows. After a big and fast success with a one-product strategy, Apple's strategy had to be updated. Steve Jobs – an innovator and electronic nerd himself – brought Apple with the new strategy into the 21st century. The new core strategy stands for: youth, modernity, premium price, simple usability and beautiful design. The mentioned products are similar all over the world.

4.4.2. Implementation on iPhone 6S Plus

The story begins in 2007, when Steve Jobs declared, that Apple is going to reinvent the
phone and presents the iPhone – a multifunctional tool, mobile phone, iPod, E-Mail and
web applications – in a small hand-sized device. Apple-Fans all over the globe were
waiting in long rows, for hours and days to get hold of an iPhone. These pictures are
constant companions of each new iPhone generation release – including the happy faces
of new owners (Wächter, 2016). Due to fast electronic development and a highly competitive environment almost every year, a new updated iPhone has been presented like
shown in Figure 7.

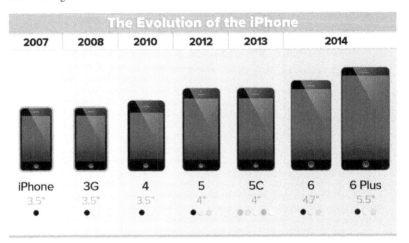

Figure 11: The Evolution of the iPhone (TheTipsGuru.com, 2016)

Not only the size of the screen, but also the size of the whole device and the diversity of
colors got higher – see Figure 7. On the other hand, the depth decreased from 12.3mm
to 7.1mm a reduction of more than 15 percent, during a percentage screen enlargement
of more than 50.

The whole product line is entirely coherent. Concerning the design, the changes concern
principally the size and the colors. More important are the intrinsic values, such as
software, operating system, camera and even more parts.

Whether it is the iPhone – 1st Generation – or the current flagship edition the iPhone 6S
Plus, with each generation Apple has its finger on the pulse. Apple's strategy – being
innovative, different and fashionable – is complied in each part by each edition. The

iPhone S6 Plus has the ageless design of its forerunners. The rounded down edges are a synonym for Apple. The company had the patent 618.677 for this characteristic as design protection until 2015, then the patent has been detracted (WEKA FACHMEDIEN GmbH, 2016).

Summarized a perfect implementation of the organization's core strategy adapted to the current-gen iPhone 6S Plus.

4.4.3. Cultural Characteristics of Product Communication on Indian Market

As mentioned in 4.3.3 the three major disturbances on the Indian smartphone market, which influence the turnover, sold devices and market share. These are the highly competitive industry, the price-performance ratio and not the brand. The brand Apple sells itself by using the cult around it, the style, the haptic, the premium-price, which is the core strategy. Exactly this is not what Indians are looking for.

This is a difficult endeavor for Apple's current-gen flagship model the iPhone 6S Plus. However, Apple already adapted the bigger screen, although it was known, that Apple formerly did not want to enlarge the size screen. Apple accepted the customers' wish contrary to own strategy. This is one of the few adaptions towards the competitors' developments.

To market the iPhone 6S Plus, which obviously does not fit into market requirements, iPhone approaches Indian culture, not in all for product communication usable mediums, but in some. On the one hand – comparable to Samsung – the Indian iPhone website is not culturally and regarding different countries not adjusted. Indeed, it is – in a different way from Samsung – not pragmatic. It is similar to the own strategy more emotional, with rotating smartphones in different colors, which may give the viewer the impression of being in a light dream, due to bright colors and short facts (Apple Inc., 2016).

On the other hand, a video commercial fully caters to Indian consumers. In this spot, an Indian couple is going to marry. They share short videos and pictures of each other's faces, parts of their dresses and what is allowed. During the unique interpersonal moment of the first sight of the opposite, the company withdraws from the focus. The commercial focuses like the website or other most commercials, within the Apple channel on YouTube, on the camera as well as on the speed the camera and the whole smartphone has (Apple, 2016).

To conclude the cultural characteristics of the iPhone 6S Plus in India, one must know Apple's strategy. The company is not able to make a U-turn to fit India's culture caused requirements and demand, which is not judgmental. Apple diverges from its own strategy by creating cultural fitting commercials combined with the emotion of a moment. This emotion is again part of the core strategy. In this way, Apple will not get implausible, although it is not a coherent implemented strategy.

4.5.   Comparison of Facts and Figures

In this section, the author illustrates the importance of the contemplated companies for economy with important facts.

In Figure 12 the chosen facts – Sales in million $US, annual ROI and employees – are compared with each other for the companies Sony in blue, Microsoft in red, Samsung in green and Apple in purple.

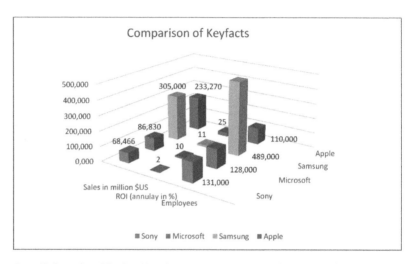

Figure 12: Comparison of Key facts (Own Figure according data of (Forbes Media LLC, 2016))

These factors affect their national as well as global economy. All three companies have common sales of approximately 700,000,000,000 $US, that is comparable to a third of India's GDP or a thirteen of China's GDP. It points the contribution of each company to the global economics out. The ROI explains the earnings one can expect by investing into mentioned companies. Besides, the ROI includes a future expectation of organizational development. All the companies except Sony have a higher ROI than China's and India's average GDP including future predictions (Figure 6).

With combined 858,000 employees, the companies are offering a job for a small city and help decreasing unemployment. Moreover, due to continuous growth of these companies the data will be developed in positive way, so that the contribution to economic will rise. Against all positive influences the companies have on economy, there increasingly power and dominance can be dangerous. The prices as well as salary can be influenced in a negative way, due to the lack of alternative suppliers or employers in several regions. Economic authorities must monitor the organizations carefully.

5. Results – Critical Discussion – Recommendation

After the company specific explanations – in the former chapters – in this section the author reviews the observations. They will be compared with each other and referred to cultural backgrounds as well as the core strategies. So that, a connection between strategic orientation and cultural environment will originate.

At first, the author gives attention to the Chinese game console market and compares the organizations Sony and Microsoft in core strategy, implementation on particular device and adaption of cultural characteristics in China.

The second step includes the Indian smartphone market with focus on the comparison of the companies Apple and Samsung as well as their core strategies, transfer of these strategies onto the smartphones and the cultural specifications in India.

The third step will consist of recommendations for more effective advertisement. More effective in the way of cultural adaption by fitting into specific cultural requirements if necessary.

The Chinese market is as already mentioned a difficult one. For both Microsoft and Sony, it is comparable to a new market entry. The sale, as well as the production of game consoles was banned by the government in 2014. These special characteristics in the market affect both market participants, as well as the advantage of common competitors computers and mobile devices, who could collect experience and customer specifications within the time period, in the technical rapidly developing industry.

As results from the monitoring of the implementation of the respective core strategies on the products and the culturally determined adaptation of product communication, the following results are obtained. Microsoft has perceived the market potential immediately and has entered the Chinese game console market rapidly. At the beginning, the Xbox started due to the restrictions with a small menu. Sony did not start immediately in China, but only half a year after Microsoft and also with a reasonable offer.

Culturally Microsoft tried to position itself with an adapted advertising and represent the far-reaching capabilities of the gaming console. In the audiovisual communication via spots, cultural change is indeed realizable; however, these are aligned stereotypically without a recognizable focus group. The pictographic representation is not adapted, but transnational conform. The concrete relationship to Microsoft's core strategy cannot be drawn entirety. On the one hand, this product, due to mentioned limitations, will definitely not achieve market dominance in China, and on the other hand, the Xbox One obviously is an innovation since the previous one due to further development and it has been extended to certain applications and innovations.

Culturally Sony has bent the censorship of government and accordingly, as well as Microsoft, few titles for the introduction of PlayStation 4 in China. The internet presence in the US or in European nations is through the video loop that runs in the background more active than the simple representation of the console on a black background (Figure 7). In terms of video, there is also little culture-specific and customized advertising. There are no cultural characteristics per se, but there are classic games shown which include the Chinese culture. Furthermore, each person is to be addressed, it is played across generations together. Even Sony cannot implement its strategy completely on the console, due to physical limitations. Possible improvements and recommendations will be summarized at the end of this chapter.

The Indian market is formed by various kinds of mobile phone vendors, so that a high market share is difficult to achieve because a single supplier is not able to fit all market and customer requirements. For Samsung, the implementation of its core strategy on the Samsung Galaxy S6 Edge+ is easier to enforce, especially taking into account the cultural adaption to the Chinese market. The preferences – good price-performance ratio, fast processor, a good camera and a good mobile network – are fulfilled. The own production plant is an advantage, as this reduces the prices by reducing costs. However, prices of the top models from Samsung – the Galaxy S series – have been rising. Culturally adapted communication cannot be found, neither the own website, nor various spots or pictures are different in diverse countries. That does not apply to individual nations, but it fits into Indian pragmatism in finding the smartphone, as all used media, communicate via facts and the actual device. A special adjustment or revision of the core strategy is also not to be recognized, because there are no intersections with cultural characteristics.

Apple's situation is slightly different. The technical requirements can Apple fulfill, but the criterion price is incompatible with its premium pricing strategy. Apple tried to circumnavigate this with culturally appropriate advertising and address this commercial to the interpersonal relationships. This route is an option and shows that the cultural adaptation is an essential tool even if it is not compatible in 100 percent of its own strategy.

Other forms of promotion, such as the own website are not or slightly adjusted, as the other companies do, too.

This global equality of these websites can be explained with the comparatively higher costs which would be generated by creating an own website for each country. Especially the smartphone market is extremely fast moving and developing and sorting of out-of-date equipment is rapid. Thus, the continuous adaptation of the sites considering cost is not efficient, in what way the standardization inhibits sales due to lack of cultural adaptation has not been verified.

The overall low number, as well as slight cultural depth can be attributed to two problems. Firstly, the aforementioned fast pace of the market is a challenge especially for the smartphone manufacturers. Within this market, the two companies should focus more on social media such as YouTube, Instagram, Facebook or Snapchat, since the focus groups communicate digital. So that a kind of digital word-of-mouth can be developed what nowadays works more efficient and faster than ever. Secondly, the situation in China is still in the exploration, due to the lift of the game console ban. So that the companies Microsoft and Sony are still in the country-specific determination. With increasing time in the Chinese market, the companies will collect experiences and these should keep in mind for future products in communication and application.

6. Conclusion and Outlook

At the end of the thesis, a conclusion on the progress of work will be drawn and the
gained knowledge will be recapitulated. An outlook on the possible future development
will be given and how to influence it.

At the beginning of the thesis, the term product communication has been deferred and
put in relation to marketing. It has been noticed that product communication is an essential part of the marketing mix. Firstly, the communication as advertising is core component to enhance the degree of brand awareness involving increasing sales. In addition,
the product is in the spotlight. The cultural adaptation in the two countries China and
India is the central question. Therefore, both countries – especially their cultures and the
respective markets – have been assessed. The various characteristics have been exposed
the main part is based on. In the main part of the thesis, the author is concerned with the
companies Sony, Microsoft, Samsung and Apple. The core strategies of the organizations have been evaluated and the various forms have been analyzed and verified for
implementation on the devices. The mentioned companies have definitely concerned
themselves with the various markets. However, this is a partly superficial examination
of the cultures, the market conditions have been examined in more detail. Thus, it can
be assessed, that – taking account of costs and efficiency – the efficacy was evaluated.
In the case of Sony and Microsoft, the situation is due to the recently abolished game
console prohibition and strong censorship, difficult to assess. To what extent invest-
ments for communication are and / or were retained is difficult to evaluate, however, the
shallow depth of the adjustment to the Chinese culture and the small number of culture-
specific communication show that the effectiveness was assessed as not large. The
strong market participants and their foreknowledge about the market and the potential
customers may be a reason. With Apple and Samsung, the results are comparable. The
communication has been adjusted in parts, but they are not completely deviated from
the standardized advertising, because neither the strategy of Samsung nor Apple's do
completely agree with the culture and market-specific conditions.

In summary, the results show that the cultural adaptation in listed global players could
not be enforced in any area. This makes sense, as the efficiency and cost must also be
considered. As soon as a company adapts its own strategy in the communication of the
products for the considered audience – here the two countries China and India – there

must be collected not only superficially information about the culture, but also with market research illuminate the market from the inside. Accordingly, the knowledge of the culture and the target group depends on the seriousness and the success of the product communication. In the adjustment of product communication, your strategy should certainly not be completely disregarded, as can have a negative effect on the credibility of the company.

In what way a cultural adaptation in the future will be needed, is difficult to conceive as the national, as well as the transcontinental borders become smaller. The Internet, social media and the powerful mobile networks offer an extremely rapid exchange between potential customers, independent of each other's location. Therefore, a focus on these media will be inevitable in the future, so that conventional advertising, like posters will be rare. The interaction between companies and customers is an interesting and cultural perfect way of inquiring other customers. The result is digital word-of-mouth that circulates rapidly. Very economic and effective. Whether and how strongly it can influence an increase in sales will be demonstrated in future.

References

9to5mac.com. (2016, July 16). *9TO5Mac*. Retrieved from Samsung remains a key
supplier for Apple's iPhone despite patent disputes, competition:
http://9to5mac.com/2015/02/24/samsung-apple-iphone-supplier/

Abhishek. (2016, July 27). *Dazeinfo*. Retrieved from Indian Smartphone Users Prefer
Scrutinizing Price And Features, Not Brand:
http://dazeinfo.com/2016/02/04/smartphone-market-india-users-preferences-
price-features/

Apfelthaler, G. (1999). *Internationale Markteintrittsstrategien: Unternehmen auf
Weltmärkten [International Marketentry-Strategies: Companies on global
markets]*. Wien: Manz-Verlag Schulbuch.

Apple. (2016, July 30). *YouTube*. Retrieved from Apple:
https://www.youtube.com/channel/UCE_M8A5yxnLfW0KghEeajjw

Apple Inc. (2016, July 30). *Apple*. Retrieved from iPhone6S:
http://www.apple.com/in/iphone-6s/

Bell, M. W., Khor, H. E., Kochhar, K., Ma, J., N'guiamba, S., & Lall, R. (1993). *China
at the Treshold of a Market Economy*. Washington DC: International Monetary
Fund.

Bidness ETC. (2016, July 2). *Bidness ETC*. Retrieved from Sony Corp Success With
PlayStation 4 Is Due To Change In Core Strategy:
http://www.bidnessetc.com/49115-sony-corp-success-with-playstation-4-is-due-
to-change-in-core-strategy/

Bundeszentrale für politische Bildung. (2016, June 24). *Bundeszentrale für politische
Bildung*. Retrieved from Die unabhängige Republik Indien - Historische
Eckpunkte und politische Entwicklungen von 1947 bis zur Gegenwart [the
Idependent Republic India - Historic basci points and political development
from 1947 until present]:
http://www.bpb.de/internationales/asien/indien/44407/geschichte-ab-1947

Cambridge Professional Academy Ltd. (2016, January 20). *Professional Academy*.
Retrieved from Marketing Theories:
http://www.professionalacademy.com/blogs-and-advice/marketing-theories---
the-marketing-mix---from-4-p-s-to-7-p-s

Chopra, A., Collyns, C., Hemming, R., Parker, K., Chu, W., & Fratzscher, O. (1995). *India: Economic Reform and Growth.* Washington DC: International Monetary Fund.

Chow, I., Holbert, N., Kelley, L., & Yu, J. (1997). *Business Strategy - An Asia-Pacific Focus.* Singapore: Simon & Schuster Pte Ltd.

Cornelissen, J. (2004). *Corporate Communications: Theory and Practice.* London: SAGE Publications Ltd.

Cushman, D. P., & Sanderson King, S. (2001). *Excellence in Communicating Organizational Strategy.* Albany: State University of New York Press.

Cusumano, M. A., & Selby, R. W. (1996). *Die Microsoft Methode: Sieben Prinzipien, wie man ein Unternehmen an die Weltspitze bringt. [The Microsoft-Method: Seven principles, how to become a come the worldleader.].* Freiburg: Rudolf Haufe Verlag.

Dalmia, V., & Sadana, R. (2012). *The Cambridge Companion to Modern Indian Culture.* Cambridge: Cambridge University Press.

de Wit, B., & Meyer, R. (2010). *Strategy - Process, Content, Context.* Cengage Learning Emea: Cambridge.

Deresky, H. (2014). *International Management - Managing Across Borders and Cultures.* Edinburgh: Pearson Education Limited.

Deutsche Zentrale für Tourismus e.V. (2016, June 25). *Deutschlad Tourismus [Germany Tourism].* Retrieved from Marktinformationen Incoming-Tourismus Deutschland 2016 - Indien [Marketinformation Incoming tourism Germany 2016 - India]: http://www.germany.travel/de/index.html

Erdmann, C. (2011). *One more thing - Apples Erfolgsgeschichte vom Apple I bis zum iPad (Apple Gadgets und OS) [One more thing - Apple's successful story from Apple I to iPad(Apple Gadgets and OS)].* München: Addison-Wesley.

Fill, C. (2001). *Marketing-Kommunikation - Konzepte und Strategien [Marketing-Communication - Concepts and Strategies].* München: Pearson Education Limited.

Fingas, J. (2016, July 23). *Engadget.* Retrieved from 'Koi' is the first PS4 game made entirely in China: https://www.engadget.com/2016/03/05/first-chinese-made-ps4-game/

Forbes Media LLC. (2016, June 12). *Forbes - The World's Biggest Public Companies.* Retrieved from Global 2000: http://www.forbes.com/global2000/

Forbes Media LLC. (2016, June 26). *Forbes Asia*. Retrieved from India Just Crossed 1
Billion Mobile Subscribers Milestone And The Excitement's Just Beginning:
http://www.forbes.com/sites/saritharai/2016/01/06/india-just-crossed-1-billion-
mobile-subscribers-milestone-and-the-excitements-just-
beginning/#981df605ac25

Framson, E. A. (2007). *Translation in der internationalen Marketingkommunikation
[Translation in international Marketingcommunication]*. Tübingen:
Stauffenburg Verlag Brigitte Narr GmbH.

Gartz, J. (2005). *Die Apple-Story. Aufstieg, Niedergang und "Wieder-Auferstehung" des
Unternehmens rund um Steve Jobs [The Apple-Story. Rise, Fall and
'Resurrection' of the Company around Steve Jobs]*. Kilchberg: SmartBooks
Publishing AG.

Gatignon, H., & Kimberly, J. R. (2016, January 26). *Cambridge University Press*.
Retrieved from The INSEAD–Wharton Alliance on Globalizing: Strategies for
Building   Successful   Global   Businesses:
http://assets.cambridge.org/97805218/35718/excerpt/9780521835718_excerpt.p
df

Griffith, E. (2016, July 24). *PCMag*. Retrieved from The Story Behind the Xbox:
http://uk.pcmag.com/game-systems-reviews/6059/feature/the-story-behind-the-
xbox

Handelsblatt GmbH. (2016, June 26). *Handelsblatt*. Retrieved from Indiens Bedeutung
wächst   [India's   Importance   grow]:
http://www.handelsblatt.com/unternehmen/mittelstand/wirtschaftsentwicklung-
indiens-bedeutung-waechst/2708194-all.html

Hearst Newspaper, LLC. (2016, February 23). *Small Business*. Retrieved from How
Effective   Communication   Will   Help   an   Organization:
http://smallbusiness.chron.com/effective-communication-organization-
1400.html

Hoffmann, C., Lennerts, S., Schmitz, C., Stölzle, W., & Uebernickel, F. (2015).
*Business Innovation: Das St. Galler Modell [Business Innovation: The St.
Galler Model]*. Wiesbaden: Springer Gabler Wiesbaden.

Hofstede, G., Van Hofstede, G., & Minkov, M. (2010). *Cultures and Organizations -
Software of the Mind: Intercultural Cooperation and Its Importance for Survival*.
New York: Mcgraw-Hill Education Ltd.

Hollensen, S. (2014). *Global Marketing - Sixth Edition.* Edinburgh Gate: Pearson Education Limited.

IKEA Deutschland GmbH & Co. KG. (2016, January 26). *Ikea.* Retrieved from Ikea: http://www.ikea.com/ms/de_DE/this-is-ikea/about-the-ikea-group/index.html

iportale GmbH. (2016, June 24). *Länder Lexikon [Country Lexikon].* Retrieved from Indien Geschichte [India History]: http://www.laender-lexikon.de/Indien_Geschichte

Jandt, F. E. (1995). *Intercultural Communication - An Introduction.* California: SAGE Publications, Inc.

Jou, E. (2016, July 26). *YouTube.* Retrieved from Xbox One China Joy : https://www.youtube.com/watch?v=knsKge7r2Po&feature=youtu.be

Lang, N.-S. (1998). *Intercultural Management in China: Synergistic Management Approaches in Sino-European and Sino-Japanese Joint Ventures.* Wiesbaden: Deutscher Universitäts-Verlag.

M., S., Vembu, S. K., Agarwal, R., Dubey, A., & Kalkotwar, V. (2013). *Successful Organizations in Action: A HANDBOOK FOR CORPORATE EXCELLENCE.* Gurgaon: PartridgeIndia.

Marshall, R. (2016, July 8). *Digital Trends.* Retrieved from THE HISTORY OF THE XBOX: http://www.digitaltrends.com/gaming/the-history-of-the-xbox/

Mendoza, M. (2016, July 25). *Tech Times.* Retrieved from Xbox One officially lands in China but gamers can't get CoD, Destiny or Halo: http://www.techtimes.com/articles/16707/20140930/xbox-one-officially-lands-in-china-but-gamers-cant-get-cod-destiny-or-halo.htm

Microsoft Corp. (2016, July 25). *Microsoft.* Retrieved from Xbox One: http://www.xbox.com/zh-CN/xbox-one?xr=shellnav

Microsoft Corp. (2016, July 25). *Microsoft.* Retrieved from Xbox One: http://www.xbox.com/en-US/xbox-one?xr=shellnav

Millward Brown. (2016, June 12). *MB Global.* Retrieved from BrandZTop 100Most Valuable Chinese Brands 2016: http://www.millwardbrown.com/BrandZ/2016/China/2016_China_Top100_Chart_EN.pdf

Musolf, N. (2008). *The Story of Micrsosoft.* Minnesota: Creative Education.

Nathan, J. (2001). *Sony - The Private Life.* New York: Mariner Books.

News Limited. (2016, June 18). *News.com.au*. Retrieved from 13 amazing facts you
never knew about Sony: http://www.news.com.au/technology/home-
entertainment/tv/13-amazing-facts-you-never-knew-about-sony/news-
story/d3ebb2fedfd6186a4495b71d6092a627

Nisen, M. (2016, July 16). *Business Insider*. Retrieved from Samsung Has A Totally
Different Strategy From Apple, And It's Working Great:
http://www.businessinsider.com/samsung-corporate-strategy-2013-3?IR=T

Office of Public Affairs. (2016, June 2). *Central Intelligence Agency*. Retrieved from
The World Factbook: https://www.cia.gov/library/publications/the-world-
factbook/geos/in.html

O'Grady, J. D. (2009). *Apple Inc*. London: Greenwood Press.

Ohga, N. (2008). *Doing It Our Way - A Sony Memoir*. Tokyo: International House of
Japan.

OnVista Group. (2016, July 18). *OnVista Mein Finanzportal*. Retrieved from Apple
Stack: http://www.onvista.de/aktien/Apple-Aktie-US0378331005

Pawan S., B. (2010). *Doing Business in India*. Florence: Routledge.

PlayStation. (2016, July 2). *Youtube*. Retrieved from PlayStation E3 Press Conference
2013 [Video File]: https://www.youtube.com/watch?v=DmoZAPDV3ew

Rodewald, A. (2007). *Business Know-How Indien - So wird Ihre Geschäftsreise zum
Erfolg [Business Know-How India - This way your business trip becomes a
success]*. Heidelberg: Redline Wirtschaft.

Rohn, U. (2010). *Cutural Barriers to the Success of Foreign Media Content - Western
Media in China, India and Japan*. Frankfurt am Main: Peter Lang GmbH.

Rohwetter, M. (2012). Samsung - Erfolg auf Befehl [Samsung- Success according
command]. *Die Zeit*.

Rosenkranz, S. (1996). *Cooperation for Product Innovation*. Berlin: Edition Sigma®
Rainer Bohn Verlag.

Samsung. (2016, July 15). *Samsung*. Retrieved from Samsung's Beginnings:
http://www.samsung.com/us/aboutsamsung/samsung_group/history/

Samsung Corp. (2016, July 28). *Samsung*. Retrieved from Samsung Galaxy S6 Edge+:
http://www.samsung.com/in/consumer/mobile-devices/smartphones/galaxy-
s/SM-G925IZDAINS

Samsung Mobile. (2016, July 27). *YouTube*. Retrieved from Samsung Galaxy S6 edge+ :
Official Introduction: https://www.youtube.com/watch?v=_Q-p-zkydLQ

Savoya Consulting UG. (2016, June 19). *YN Yelling News*. Retrieved from Sony Playstation: https://www.yellingnews.com/konsole/sony-playstation.html

Schmid, S. (2006). *Strategien der Internationalisierung: Fallstudien und Fallbeispiele [Strategies of Internationlyzing: Case-Studies and Case-Examples]*. München: Oldenbourg Wissenschaftsverlag GmbH.

Schönenstein, J. (2015, November 11). *Communicode*. Retrieved from Andere Märkte - Andere Sitten - Andere Länder - Andere Produkte [Other Markets - Other Conventions - Other Countries - Other Products]: https://www.communicode.de/img_global/communicode_fachartikel_andere_m aerkte_andere_sitten.pdf

Shater, R. (2012, January 1). Intercultural New Media Studies: The Next Frontier in intercultural Communication. *Journal of Intercultural Communication Research*, pp. 219-237.

Siebenhaar, L. (2016, July 16). *All about Samsung*. Retrieved from Evolution of Samsung: Die Geschichte von Samsung als Infografik [Evolution of Samsung: The Story of Samsung as Picture]: https://allaboutsamsung.de/2013/04/evolution-of-samsung-die-geschichte-von-samsung-als-infografik/

Sony Interactive Entertainment LLC. (2016, July 23). *Sony PlayStation*. Retrieved from Overview: https://www.playstation.com/en-us/explore/ps4/?smcid=sony:us:pdp:playstation:gwt_pdp_visit:playstation:ps

Sony Interactive Entertainment LLC. (2016, July 23). *Sony PlayStation*. Retrieved from Overview: http://www.playstation.com.cn/ps4/Dynasty-Warriors-8-Empire/ps4-feature.htm

Statista GmbH. (2016, June 26). *statista*. Retrieved from Indien: Anteile der Wirtschaftssektoren am Bruttoinlandsprodukt (BIP) von 2004 bis 2014 [India: Shares of economic sectors of Gross Domestic Product (GDP) from 2004 until 2014]: http://de.statista.com/statistik/daten/studie/170838/umfrage/anteile-der-wirtschaftssektoren-am-bruttoinlandsprodukt-indiens/

StatisticsTimes.com. (2016, June 25). *Statistics Times*. Retrieved from India vs China GDP: http://statisticstimes.com/economy/china-vs-india-gdp.php

Statistisches Bundesamt. (2016, March 18). *Destatis - Statisches Bundesamt [Destatis - Statistic Federal Office]*. Retrieved from Länderprofil China [National Profile of China]:

https://destatis.de/DE/ZahlenFakten/LaenderRegionen/Internationales/Land/Asie
n/China.html

TheTipsGuru.com. (2016, July 20). *TheTipsGuru.com*. Retrieved from The Story of
Apple's   Smartphone   –iPhone: http://thetipsguru.com/wp-
content/uploads/2015/09/ios-8-adoption-iphone-evolution.jpg

Thompson, J. (2001). *Understanding Corporate Strategy*. London: Thomson Learning.

Thomson Reuters. (2016, July 3). *Reuters*. Retrieved from Sony says China sales of
PlayStation 4 limited by censorship rules: http://www.reuters.com/article/us-
sony-playstation-china-idUSKCN0RH0IN20150917

Times Internet Limited. (2016, July 27). *The Economic Times*. Retrieved from Samsung,
Micromax,   Intex   lead   Indian   smartphone   market   in   Q4:
http://economictimes.indiatimes.com/tech/hardware/samsung-micromax-intex-
lead-indian-smartphone-market-in-q4/articleshow/52214296.cms

Tribune Publishing. (2016, June 12). *LA Times*. Retrieved from China's open gaming-
console   market   may   not   mean   much   for   Microsoft   and   Sony:
http://www.latimes.com/business/technology/la-fi-tn-china-consoles-20150727-
story.html

Troester, M. (2016, June 18). *Encyclopedia*. Retrieved from Sony Corporation:
http://www.encyclopedia.com/topic/Sony_Corp.aspx

Vox Media. (2016, June 19). *The Verge*. Retrieved from The history of the Walkman:
35   years   of   iconic   music   players:
http://www.theverge.com/2014/7/1/5861062/sony-walkman-at-35

Wächter, M. (2016). *Mobile Strategy: Marken- und Unternehmensführung im Angesicht
des Mobile Tsunami [Mobile Strategy: Brand and Business Management in
contemplation of the Mobile Tsunami]*. Wiesbaden: Springer Gabler.

Wala, H. H. (2011). *Meine Marke - Was Unternehmen authentisch, unverwechselbar
und langfristig erfolgreich macht [My Brand - What is it that make companies
authentic, noninterchangeable and long-term successful]*. München: Redline
Verlag.

Weiber, R. (1993). *Was ist Marketing? Ein informationsökonomischer
Erklärungsansatz [What is marketing? An information-economic explanation
approach]*. Trier: Univ.-Prof.-Dr. Rolf Weiber.

WEKA FACHMEDIEN GmbH. (2016, July 20). *CRN*. Retrieved from Design-Schutz
für iPhone und iPad nichtig: Apple-Patent auf »runde Ecken« aberkannt

[Design-Protection for iPhone and iPad void: Apple-Patent for 'rounded Edges' denied]: http://www.crn.de/telekommunikation/artikel-107664.html

White, C. (2004). *Strategic Management.* Houndmills Basingstoke: Palgrave Macmillan.

Youku. (2016, July 25). *Youku.* Retrieved from 视频: 百事通 X 微软，XBOX ONE 中国版宣传片[Video: X Knowing Microsoft, XBOX ONE China Version trailer trade Fair Version A]: http://v.youku.com/v_show/id_XNTYwMzUzNDg4.html?from=y1.2-1-99.4.1-1.1-1-2-0-0%26source%3Dautoclick

ZhugeEx. (2016, July 23). *YouTube.* Retrieved from PS4 HD Commercial for China: https://www.youtube.com/watch?v=ay_pa6p1qOk

ZhugeEx. (2016, July 22). *ZhugeEx Blog.* Retrieved from Legal sales of PS4 & XB1 to exceed 1 million in China: https://zhugeex.com/2016/07/legal-sales-of-ps4-xb1-to-exceed-1-million-in-china/

Zinzius, B. (1996). *China Business - Der Ratgeber zur erfolgreichen Unternehmensführung [China Business - The Guideline for Successful Business Management].* Wiesbaden: Gabler.

YOUR KNOWLEDGE HAS VALUE